LOVELAND PUE

00054
D0114052

5/15
95
ET
15

Withdrawn

GAMES for all the FAMILY

GAMES FOR ALL THE FAMILY

Copyright © Summersdale Publishers Ltd, 2013

Text contributed by Emily Kearns

All rights reserved.

No part of this book may be reproduced by any means, nor transmitted, nor translated into a machine language, without the written permission of the publishers.

Condition of Sale
This book is sold subject to the condition that it shall not, by way of trade or otherwise, be lent, re-sold, hired out or otherwise circulated in any form of binding or cover other than that in which it is published and without a similar condition including this condition being imposed on the subsequent purchaser.

Summersdale Publishers Ltd
46 West Street
Chichester
West Sussex
PO19 1RP
UK

www.summersdale.com

Printed and bound in the Czech Republic

ISBN: 978-1-84953-471-0

Substantial discounts on bulk quantities of Summersdale books are available to corporations, professional associations and other organisations. For details contact Nicky Douglas by telephone: +44 (0) 1243 756902, fax: +44 (0) 1243 786300 or email: nicky@summersdale.com.

GAMES
for all the
FAMILY

Harry Hilton

summersdale

For Charlotte, Nick and Zander –
Slam champions of the 1990s

Contents

LET THE GAMES BEGIN!

Old-fashioned fun has a tendency to bring people together. Remember your last power cut? When the candles were brought out and anything that required a wall socket to provide entertainment suddenly became useless? As we become ever more reliant on digital means of amusement, sometimes we need a nudge to take a moment, turn off our mobiles and put the iPad in a drawer along with the TV remote control.

Most of the games in the pages that follow can be played with little more than a pen and paper or a pack of cards, and sometimes even those aren't required. It's time to remember that old-fashioned fun doesn't have to be old-fashioned; it's our job to keep the after-dinner gaming spirit alive for generations to come – and I'm not talking about *Mario Kart*.

Consequences, which requires no more than a gaggle of friends and family, an over-active imagination and some writing implements, will have everyone howling with laughter. Capture the Flag merely calls for a tea towel and an open space, but will provide ample room for family bonding, as an overriding sense of teamwork propels the winning team to the podium. Feel the frantic rush of competition as you battle it out at Slam or Back to the Drawing Board, and exercise your grey matter with a round of Botticelli – where everybody takes something away from the table, be it a host of new facts or the smug face of victory.

Best of all, these games are free. In these times of austerity we could all do with knocking a few quid off the electricity bill, so switch off the TV and embrace some good old-fashioned fun.

CARD GAMES

Go Fish!

Who will escape with the bait?

No. of players required: Three or more

Aim of the game: To collect as many four of a kinds as you possibly can

Card Games

How to start: This is a good one to play when you have plenty of table space. Give the cards a good shuffle and deal five cards to each player (or seven cards if there are fewer than four players). Take the remaining cards, give them another healthy shuffle and spread them out face down in the middle of the table (which is the 'sea'). There's no order here – they can be in a big messy pile, as long as no one can see what they are.

The simple part: Choose a player to start – it's often easiest to start with the youngest. The starting player should assess the cards in their hand and ask one of the other players for a type of card; but they must already have a card of that kind to request one. For example, they might say, 'Do you have any aces?' but they must have an ace in their hand to ask the question. Honesty is important in Go Fish! If you hold a card in your hand that has been requested by another player you must give it up. If they are successful, their turn continues; if they are unsuccessful, the player asking will be told to 'Go Fish!' and must select a card from the 'sea' in front of them. Once you have collected four of a kind (for example, aces, threes, etc.), you must place the cards face up in a pile in front of you. The game continues until a player has got rid of all their cards and the winner is the player with the most sets of four. Don't be the player who doesn't catch any fish!

Slam

Are you fast enough to speed to victory?

No. of players required: Two

Aim of the game: To get rid of all your cards as quickly as possible

How to start: Quite possibly the most energetic card game there is, Slam is not for the faint-hearted. Take a pack of cards and give it a thorough shuffle. Split the pack exactly in half, so each player has 26 cards. Each player lays four cards face down in a row in front of them and one face up at the end; then three face down on top of the separate cards and one face up on the fourth card; continue this, laying two face down and the third face up, one face down and the second face up and then one card face up on the first pile. Before the game begins, assess the piles of cards in front of you. If you have any cards of the same rank, for example, queens or threes, these can be placed on top of each other to open up new cards. Place the remaining cards in two separate piles in between the two players.

The simple part: Shout 'Go!' and each player should turn over the first card from their pile in the middle – these are your 'starting cards'. The aim is to then build on that card by following it with a card with a higher or lower value of one – for example, if it is a four you can follow it with a three or a five, if it is a king you can follow it with a queen or an ace – building and building as fast as you can (on either pile) until neither of you can go. Then turn over another starting card from the pile and start building again. The first to get rid of all of their cards must slam their hand onto the smallest pile in the middle, which they then take, along with their pile of starting cards, and set up their cards as before. Once there are not enough cards for a player to complete the set-up, the other player must supply a 'slam card', which will win them the game if they get rid of all their cards and smack their hand onto it. Be warned, though, any player can go for the slam card and all manners are left at the starting block in this game. Some versions state only one hand can be used to make this all the more challenging.

Pig

The most eagle-eyed piggies will triumph in this game

No. of players required: Four or more

Aim of the game: To be the first player to collect four of a kind

How to start: In Pig you can have as many players as you like and if the numbers top 13 you may need to incorporate another deck of cards into the mix. This is best played when everyone sits around a table or in a circle. Choose someone to be dealer and reduce the pack to the number of players multiplied by four, so there are as many sets of four cards as there are players. Shuffle the cards thoroughly and deal four cards to each player.

The simple part: Players must select one card from the four they were dealt and, all at the same time, slide it face down on the table/floor to the player on their left. This continues until one of the players has successfully collected four of a kind. This player must then place their finger on their nose (snout) and sit quietly while the other players notice and follow suit. The last player to put their finger on their nose is given the letter 'P'. On the next round that player loses they are given the letter 'I'. Play rounds until someone has spelt the word 'Pig' or, for longer games, try 'Pigs', 'Piglet' or Piglets' and keep playing until there is only one player without a full word; they will be the ultimate winner!

Did you know?

The King of Hearts is the only king in a deck of cards without a moustache.

Spoons

No. of players required: Four or more

What you will need: A pack of cards and one spoon fewer than there are players

The simple part: Reduce the pack to as many sets of four as there are players and deal four cards to each player. Everyone should pass one card, face down, to their left at the same time, until someone collects a set of four. They should then subtly reach for a spoon and place it in front of them. The last player to follow suit is left empty handed and is out. Remove a spoon per round.

Old Maid

No. of players required: Two or more

What you will need: A pack of cards with all but one of the queens removed. Traditionally, the Old Maid is the Queen of Spades.

The simple part: Once all the cards have been dealt, players should assess their hand and remove any pairs they have, putting the cards in the centre of the table. Take it in turns to pick a card from the hand of the player to your left – without looking – then assess your new hand, discarding any pairs as you go along. The aim is to give the queen, who is lurking somewhere, to another player. Whoever ends up with the queen loses the game.

Cheat

No. of players required: Three or more

What you will need: A pack of cards and a good poker face

The simple part: Deal out all the cards. Players take it in turns to place up to four cards of the same rank face down in the centre and announce what they are – but they don't have to tell the truth; it's up to the other players to decide. Cards should be played in sequence. For example, the first player might say 'two aces' – the next player must then put down kings or twos. If you suspect a player, shout 'Cheat!' and check the cards they have just put down – if you are right, they must pick up the whole pile, but if you have accused them incorrectly then that pile is yours. The winner is the first to get rid of all of their cards.

Go Boom!

No. of players required: Three or more

What you will need: A pack of cards and a heap of luck

The simple part: Deal seven cards face down to each player and place the remaining cards in the centre – this is the pick-up pile. The starting player should place any card face up next to the pick-up pile. Players must then follow suit or rank and if they cannot, must pick up until they can. The cards from that round are then put to the bottom of the pile in the centre. The winner is the first player to get rid of all of their cards.

Beggar My Neighbour

No. of players required: Two

What you will need: A pack of cards

The simple part: Shuffle the pack and divide between the two players. Each player should hold their pile face down and take it in turns to place a card face up in the centre until one of the four 'pay cards' is played – jack requires a payment of one card; queen, two; king, three and ace, four. For example, should a player place a queen in the middle, the other player must put down two cards and, unless one of them is another pay card, the player with the queen wins the pile. Whoever ends up with all the cards wins the game.

Snap!

No. of players required: Two

What you will need: A pack of cards and an eagle eye

The simple part: As this is one of the simplest card games there is, why not shake things up and play at great speed? Split the pack in half, hold your pile face down and take it in turns to place a card face up in the centre. Whenever cards of the same rank are placed on top of each other, the first player to shout 'Snap!' wins the pile. Whoever ends up with all of the cards at the end claims victory.

Pontoon

No. of players required: Two or more

What you will need: A pack of cards and a risk-taking streak

The simple part: Choose someone to be dealer and place two cards face down in front of each player. On your go, turn over both of your cards; the aim here is to get as close to twenty-one as possible, asking the dealer for further cards by saying 'twist'. If you have two cards of the same rank you can 'split' them, placing the cards face up separately and have two turns, adding to each; if your cards add up to fourteen you can 'burn' them and ask the dealer for a new hand; royal cards are worth ten and an ace is worth one or eleven – it's up to the player. As soon as your hand exceeds twenty-one you are 'bust' and out of the game.

Sevens

No. of players required: Three or more

What you will need: A pack of cards and to be on the ball

The simple part: Deal out the whole pack and whoever has the seven of diamonds must place it in the centre and, if they can, add to the sequence in suit with either the six or eight of diamonds, until they can't place any more cards. Any further sevens should be placed in the centre next to the first one and players take turns to build on the sequences, from ace to king, until all suits are complete. The winner is whoever gets rid of all of their cards first.

Did you know?

The Guinness World Record holder for the world's tallest house of cards is Bryan Berg, who used 2,400 packs of cards to build his winning tower – 25 feet tall!

Dice Games

Everest

Strive for the summit in this game of chance

No. of players required: Two or more

Aim of the game: To be the first to throw twenty-four dice combinations adding up to a list of given numbers

How to start: Take a piece of paper each and divide it into two columns – in one column write the numbers one to twelve in ascending order and in the other twelve to one in descending order. This is your score sheet.

The simple part: For this game you will need two dice – players take it in turns to throw the dice, adding up the two numbers and crossing off the number on their list that corresponds to the total. Whoever crosses off all of their numbers first is the winner. But, remember, all numbers must exactly match the totals of the dice throw. If you want to make things a bit more challenging, enforce a rule where the columns of numbers must be crossed off in order.

Yacht

Sail your way to the top spot

No. of players required: Two or more

Aim of the game: To be the first to throw all the dice combinations on your score sheet.

How to start: Take five dice, a shaker, some paper and a pen each. First you will need to draw up a score sheet each. You may recognise this game – more commonly referred to these days as its branded counterpart Yahtzee.

Draw two columns with the headings 'Trick' and 'Score'. In the left-hand column write the tricks: Yacht (five of a kind), big straight (2, 3, 4, 5), little straight (1, 2, 3, 4), four of a kind, full house (three of a kind plus two of a kind), choice (add up dice total), sixes, fives, fours, threes, twos, ones. Yacht scores 50 points and big and little straights score 30 points each; for all other tricks simply add up the total of the dice.

The simple part: Take it in turns to throw all five dice; you are permitted three throws per turn and can save as many dice as you wish after the first roll. The idea is to fill in your entire score sheet, all the while trying to obtain the maximum points possible per trick.

Hot Dice

You'll turn up the heat when you roll high

No. of players required: Two or more

Aim of the game: To achieve the highest score possible

How to start: For this game you will need six dice and a cup, as well as a piece of paper and a pen to keep score. The scoring is as follows: a one scores 100; a five scores fifty; three ones score 1,000; three twos, 200; three threes, 300; three fours, 400; three fives, 500 and three sixes 600.

The simple part: Players should take it in turns to roll all six dice; after the first throw, at least one scoring die must be set aside, or 'banked'. After that first throw, the player must decide whether it is worth banking the score from all six dice and having it recorded, or carrying on and throwing the remaining dice in an attempt to better it. Once the initial die or dice have been set aside, no more dice can be banked. They may re-roll the remaining dice up to three times while attempting to achieve the highest score possible. If all six dice thrown are eligible for points, you have 'hot dice' and are entitled to bank those points and have another turn. Each further roll of the dice must score points, otherwise the player scores zero for that round.

Did you know?

The opposite sides of a die always add up to seven.

Fifty

No. of players required: Two or more

What you will need: Two dice, a piece of paper and a pen

The simple part: Players take it in turns to roll both dice, add the two numbers together and make a note of the score. The aim of this game is to be the first player to get to fifty. Make things more challenging and play to a hundred, or enforce a rule that you have to hit the number exactly.

Hearts

No. of players required: Two or more

What you will need: Six dice, a piece of paper and a pen

The simple part: Named so because it used to be played with lettered dice that spelt 'hearts', this game is just as easily played with numbers. Players take it in turns to throw all six dice and keep score. The scores are as follows: 1 (H) = 5 points; 1, 2 (HE) = 10 points; 1, 2, 3

(HEA) = 15 points; 1, 2, 3, 4 (HEAR) = 20 points; 1, 2, 3, 4, 5 (HEART) = 25 points; 1, 2, 3, 4, 5, 6 (HEARTS) = 35 points. If any two numbers show up more than once in a round, only one is counted, with the exception of ones – if three are thrown the player's entire score is wiped and they must start again! Play ten rounds and whoever has the highest score wins.

Newmarket

No. of players required: Three or more

What you will need: Three dice, a piece of paper and a pen

The simple part: Players take it in turns to roll all three dice. The die showing the highest number should be left on the table and the other dice rolled again; the highest of these two should be left and the final die rolled once more. Then add up the three dice and record the score. Decide at the start how many rounds you are going to play. Whoever has the highest score at the end wins the game.

Blackjack

No. of players required: Two or more

What you will need: One die, a piece of paper and a pen

The simple part: Take it in turns to roll the die, as many times as you like, until the total adds up to twenty-one. But be careful – if your total exceeds twenty-one you're 'bust' and score nothing for that round. Mark down each player's total for every round and add up at the end – whoever has the highest score wins.

Ship, Captain and Crew

No. of players required: Two or more

What you will need: Five dice, a piece of paper and a pen

The simple part: In this game, the aim is to roll a six (the 'Ship'), a five (the 'Captain') and a four (the 'Crew') in the same round. Players are entitled to three rolls to reach this goal and, once they have, the dice total is added up including the two remaining dice. If players fail to 'collect' all three, whichever they have collected are added up, but the score of the remaining dice is not added to their total for that round. Play best of five or ten and keep score; the highest score wins.

Chicago

No. of players required: Two or more

What you will need: Two dice, a piece of paper and a pen

The simple part: Many of these dice games can easily be played while travelling; this might be a good one for a train or plane journey. This is a game of eleven rounds. In each round players must attempt, in one throw, to achieve a total of two, then three, then four and so on, up to twelve. If a player is successful, they score the total of the dice; if they are not they score nothing.

Drop Dead

No. of players required: Two or more

What you will need: Five dice, a piece of paper and a pen

The simple part: Players take it in turns to throw all five dice. Twos and fives score nothing and, if thrown, are removed. The player should then continue to throw the remaining dice, removing twos and fives whenever they are rolled and adding the total of the remaining dice. When the player is left with just one die, they throw it once and take the score; however, if they throw a two or a five on their final go, they 'drop dead' and score nothing for that round.

Knockout

No. of players required: Two or more

What you will need: Two dice, a piece of paper and a pen

The simple part: Before every round each player must choose a 'knockout number' – either six, seven, eight or nine. Players then take it in turns to roll the dice – if you throw your chosen number you are out of the round, however, if you successfully avoid it you may add up the dice total and record your score. Play five or ten rounds and whoever has the highest score wins.

Did you know?

The circular dots on a die are called pips.

WORD GAMES

Consequences

*Expect the unexpected in this
scenario-building game*

No. of players required: Three or more

Aim of the game: To create the most amusing short
stories possible by taking it in turns to add the different
elements. The more familiar the players are with the
people and places, the funnier the game is.

How to start: Take a piece of paper each that is big enough to be folded over six times. At the top of the piece of paper, write a male name (this can be any old name, but it's a lot more fun to put someone you all know or a famous person/character), then fold the paper over and pass it to the player on your left. Next write a female name, fold the paper over and pass to your left.

The simple part: Continue in this way until you have completed 'where they met', 'what he said to her', 'what she said to him' and 'the consequence' (i.e. what happened). Then pass to your left and players take it in turns to smooth out the sheet of paper and read out the story – cue likely guffawing and possible sliding off chairs in merriment.

Dictionary Definitions

*Put on your best bluffing face in this game
of hilarious nonsense*

No. of players required: Four or more

Aim of the game: To outsmart your fellow competitors
with weird and wonderful definitions of unusual words

How to start: For this game you'll need a dictionary
(a book, not an online dictionary), some paper and a
pen each. Players take it in turns to sit in 'dictionary
corner', where they choose a word they suspect no one
knows; they must announce the word to the group and
if anyone knows the true meaning they should speak up
and another word will be selected.

The simple part: Whoever has the dictionary should write down the true definition of the chosen word on their scrap of paper, while the other players write down a made-up one. The aim here is to convince the other players that your definition is the correct one, so have a good think before you commit your attempt to paper – if you can also make it amusing that's a bonus. The holder of the dictionary should then gather the 'definitions' from players and shuffle them, along with the true definition, before reading them all out. Players then guess which they believe to be the true meaning of the word – whoever guesses correctly scores a point and if any players guess someone else's 'definition', the writer scores one point per correct guess.

Word Association

*Any child of the 1980s will
remember this fondly*

No. of players required: Two or more

Aim of the game: To keep up the rapid responses and
steer clear of hesitation or repetition. Children of the
1980s will remember this game a little more fondly as
Mallett's Mallet – if you have a foam hammer to hand,
now's the time to use it!

How to start: Choose a word to start – this can be
anything, but for explanation's sake, we'll say 'tiger'. The
players take it in turns to say a word associated in some
way with the preceeding word. An exchange between the
two players might go something like this: 'tiger', 'lion', 'cub',
'scout', 'brownie', 'rainbow', 'TV', 'Mad Men', 'New York',
'apple', 'orange', 'wotsit'... and so on! The possibilities are
pretty much endless and you can revisit a subject in the
same round, as long as you don't repeat a word. Players
are 'out' if they hesitate or repeat a word. The aim is to
be the last player standing.

The simple part: It's all about speed in this game. Keep things flowing as quickly as you possibly can and punish hesitation of more than three seconds. The rounds tend to work best between just two people, but you could feasibly play this with a whole table of people. Keep score and whoever claims the most rounds is victorious.

Did you know?

Mallet's Mallet was a popular feature of the 1980s Children's Saturday morning TV show Wacaday. Contestants would be hit over the head with a pink foam mallet if they stumbled when playing the word association game. Presenter Timmy Mallet once hit Margaret Thatcher over the head with the famous mallet.

Categories

No. of players required: Two or more

What you will need: Some paper, a newspaper and a pen each

The simple part: Choose four categories each – for example, countries, cheeses, musicians, vegetables – and write them in a column on the left-hand side of the paper. Choose a letter at random by dropping your finger onto the page of a newspaper with your eyes shut. Players must then write one answer per category beginning with that letter. The first to finish shouts 'stop!' and they win the round. Play best of five or ten rounds and come up with a longer list of categories if you want to make things more challenging.

Backwards Spelling

No. of players required: Three or more

What you will need: A sharp mind and a keen vocabulary

The simple part: Take it in turns to spell out words backwards, while the other players attempt to guess the word. Start with shorter words and build up to the longer ones once everyone has got in to the swing of things. Each correct guess scores a point.

Rhyming Words

No. of players required: Two or more

What you will need: To be on the ball

The simple part: This is a great game to play while on a long walk – it'll keep everyone entertained. Players take it in turns to choose a one- or two-syllable word; play then moves to their left and the next player must quickly come up with a word that rhymes. For example, 'Meat', 'heat', 'beat', 'cheat...' etc. No repetition and no hesitation! The quickest rhymer wins the round; why not play best of five?

Compound Words and Phrases

No. of players required: Two or more

What you will need: Just yourselves and some swift thinking

The simple part: Start by offering up a compound word or phrase and take it in turns to follow it with the second element and a new one, for example, 'Horseriding' could then be followed by 'riding crop', which could be followed by 'crop top', which could be followed by 'top hat', which could be followed by 'hat trick' and so on. Whoever runs out of steam first loses the round.

DIY Boggle

No. of players required: Two or more

What you will need: Some paper, a pen each, a hat or bowl and a timer

The simple part: Everyone has a timer on their mobile phone these days so this is a good game if you only have some paper and a pen. Write the letters A to Z on 26 scraps of paper, making two or three sets, and place into a hat, or bowl. Select sixteen scraps of paper each and lay out in a four lines of four; set two minutes on the timer and each player should take a separate sheet of paper and scribble down as many words of three letters or more as they can find in the grid – but remember, the letters must touch each other either horizontally, vertically or diagonally.

Song Titles

No. of players required: Two or more

What you will need: Some scraps of paper and a pen each, and a timer

The simple part: Write down some themes on some scraps of paper, for example, countries/places, animals, colours, fruit, etc., and place in a hat, or bowl. Take it in turns to select a theme from the hat and give yourselves two minutes to come up with as many song titles that relate to the theme as possible. For example, if the theme was countries you could have 'Africa', 'A New England', 'Born in the USA', 'Walk Like an Egyptian', etc. Count how many you come up with and keep score.

The 100-Word Challenge

No. of players required: Two or more

What you will need: Some paper and a pen each, and perhaps a dictionary in case people get adventurous

The simple part: Players must all attempt to write a 100-word story without repeating a word. So each word must be unique from the others and the story has to make sense, but it can be as odd as you like. Go!

A Word Within a Word

No. of players required: Two or more

What you will need: Some paper and a pen each

The simple part: Pick a theme, for example, animals. The aim of the game is to come up with as many words as possible that contain animal names within them. So you could have 'Cathedral', 'Dogma', 'Benevolent', 'Rant', 'Ballbearing' etc. Whoever comes up with the most in a minute is the winner.

Taboo

No. of players required: Two or more

What you will need: Some scraps of paper and a pen

The simple part: Write some very common words on the scraps of paper – for example, 'and', 'the', 'I', 'yes', 'no' – and place into a hat, or bowl. Each player must select a word from the hat – this word is now taboo for them. Players take it in turns to question each other on any subject, trying to provoke an answer that includes the 'taboo' word. The player in the hot seat must answer the questions in full sentences without saying the forbidden word. Once a player says their word, they're out and play continues without them. The winner is the last person to have not said their word. Make things even more challenging with forbidden letters.

Stairway

No. of players required: Two or more

What you will need: A piece of paper, a pen and a timer – and perhaps a dictionary

The simple part: Here's a good way to exercise your grey matter. Choose a letter, for example, 'T', and write it down. Now set the timer for one minute and the challenge begins – you must then write a two-letter word beginning with 'T', for example, 'to', then a three-letter word, for example, 'ten', then a four-letter word, and so on, until the timer beeps. Whoever has got the farthest up the 'stairway' wins. Check any suspicious-looking words in the dictionary.

Anagrams

No. of players required: Two or more

What you will need: A piece of paper and a pen

The simple part: Take it in turns to think of a word – six- to eight-letter words would be good to begin with –

and write the letters, jumbled up, on a piece of paper. The other players must race to guess the word comprised of the letters swimming before them and be the first to shout it out. Each correct guess scores a point.

Did you know?

The longest word ever to appear in an English language dictionary is pneumonoultramicroscopicsilicovolcanoconiosis – which is a lung condition. It's closely followed by floccinaucinihilipilification (the estimation of something as useless) and antidisestablishmentarianism (the opposition to the disestablishment of the church).

Picture Consequences

Make your friends cry with laughter

No. of players required: Three or more

Aim of the game: To create the funniest picture in three parts. There is no outright winner in picture consequences – if it makes you laugh, the game has been a success!

How to start: Take a piece of paper each and a pen. Make sure the paper is of a decent enough size for you to exercise your creativity and try to make sure all the pens are the same colour. From the top, fold the paper into three equal sections and then flatten it out – now you have your drawing boundaries set out.

The simple part: Each player should draw a head in the top section. Be as creative/wacky/odd as you like – whether human or animal, let your pen do the talking. Then you need to fold over this section of paper, so just the bottom of the neck is visible, and pass it to the player on your left. Now you need to draw the middle section of the body – add as much detail as you can – before folding the paper to hide your handiwork and passing it to the player on your left. The final section of the paper is for the legs and, once you've drawn your set, you pass the folded up consequence to your left a final time. Players should take it in turns to open the finished masterpieces, presenting them to the rest of the group and no doubt falling off chairs with laughter in the process.

Beetle

It's a creepy-crawly race to the finish

No. of players required: Two or more

Aim of the game: To be the first to 'collect' all the body parts of a beetle

How to start: You will need several sheets of paper, some pens, a counter (a bottle top will do) each and a die. Take one of the pieces of paper, draw a circle on it and divide it into six 'slices' – this is your board, so feel free to use cardboard if you have some to hand. Label the slices 'head', 'body', 'leg', 'eye', 'feelers' and 'tail'.

The simple part: Take it in turns to roll the die and move your counter around the circle – when you land on a beetle body part, you may draw it on your piece of paper. The only catch here is that you must do it in a certain order. In order to add the legs or tail you must already have the body, and to add the eyes or feelers you must already have the head. If you're competing against younger players, you can always discard the order rule to make things simpler. The winner is the first to draw a full beetle, which should be composed of one head, one body, two eyes, two feelers and six legs. Why not play best of three?

Hangman

Can you survive this classic rainy-day game?

No. of players required: Two

Aim of the game: To guess your opponent's word without meeting a grizzly end

How to start: Take a piece of paper and a pen. Think of something – be it a film, TV programme, song, band or phrase – that your opponent has to guess and draw spaces for each letter on the piece of paper. For example, if you chose the film *Toy Story*, the spaces might look like this: _ _ _ / _ _ _ _ _. Tell your opponent the theme of the round; they must then guess the answer, letter by letter.

The simple part: For every incorrect letter they guess, you draw a part of the hangman's scaffold – starting with a horizontal line for the ground, followed by a vertical line coming out of the ground, then a horizontal line to the right at the top of that and a diagonal line across the corner; then, one body part at a time, you draw a hanged stick person. If you haven't guessed correctly by this stage, I'm afraid you have lost your turn. This game sounds rather grim in this day and age, but it's a pen-and-paper classic and can be played anywhere.

Did you know?

The game Hangman dates back to nineteenth-century England when public executions were more common.

Sprouts

No. of players required: Two or more

What you will need: A piece of paper and a pen each

The simple part: Many of these drawing games, Sprouts included, are great for keeping children entertained after dinner. Draw six dots on a piece of paper and take it in turns to connect two dots with a line or connect a dot to itself with a loop, which counts as one line; then add a new dot somewhere along the line that has just been drawn. The rules of sprouts are that no line may cross another (or itself), no line may be drawn through a dot and each dot may only have three lines leading to it. The last player able to make a legitimate move wins.

Mirror Drawing

No. of players required: Four or more

What you will need: Either a large mirror or several small ones, paper and pens

The simple part: Write down a few things or objects on pieces of paper and place in a hat or bowl. Get into pairs and assign an 'artist'. Each artist should choose a piece of paper and has one minute to draw the object while their partner guesses – but the artist is only allowed to draw while looking in a mirror. This is likely to have hilarious results.

Back to the Drawing Board

No. of players required: Three or more

What you will need: A blank flip chart would be ideal – but a large sheet of paper and a surface will do – and some pens and smaller scraps of paper

The simple part: Write down as many objects/animals/places etc. as you can on the scraps of paper and place them in a hat or bowl. Each player takes a turn at the flip chart, drawing whatever is on the scrap of paper for the others to guess. The aim is to collect as many correct guesses as possible in one minute. Keep score to see who wins the game.

Alphabet Landscape

No. of players required: Two or more

What you will need: Some paper and a pen each

The simple part: This game can keep players of all ages occupied and cause much merriment. Each participant should draw a basic landscape on their piece of paper before going through the entire alphabet and adding something beginning with each letter, in order from A to Z, to their picture. Make things more interesting by introducing different landscape settings, such as outer space, underwater or on a tropical island.

Scribble

No. of players required: Two or more – and someone to judge

What you will need: Some paper and a pen each

The simple part: Each player should take a piece of paper and draw a scribble on it. Draw it however you like, but it shouldn't really look like anything and shouldn't take up the *whole* page. Then pass your scribble to the left and let your opponents' creative juices flow. The idea is to turn the scribble into something that an impartial judge will recognise.

SOS

No. of players required: Two

What you will need: A piece of paper and a pen each, and a coin

The simple part: Draw a grid of ten by ten squares – or more if you fancy a longer game. Toss a coin to see who goes first. Players should write either 'S' or 'O' (it's up to them) in any square on the grid and the aim is to get 'SOS' running horizontally, vertically or diagonally, drawing a line through it when complete and keeping score. A successful SOS warrants another go and the game continues until the grid is full.

The Strangest Story

No. of players required: Four or more

What you will need: Some paper and a pen each

The simple part: Players should take a sheet of paper and write a silly/strange sentence on it, for example: 'The giraffe sunbathed with Father Christmas' or 'Elvis thought the moon was made of cheese'. The paper should then be passed left, so the next player can illustrate it. The original sentence should then be folded over and the paper passed left so the next player can interpret the drawing. The drawing should then be folded over so the next player can interpret the sentence, and so on until you have run out of paper.

The One-Line Drawing

No. of players required: Four or more

What you will need: Some paper and a pen each, and a hat or bowl

The simple part: Write some objects/animals/places on some scraps of paper and place in a hat or bowl. Get into pairs and assign an 'artist'. The artist should choose a piece of paper from the 'hat' and draw for their partner – but without lifting the pen from the page. The winner is the team with the most correct guesses.

Three-Dimensional Noughts and Crosses

No. of players required: Two

What you will need: A piece of paper and a pen each

The simple part: This twist on a classic brings a bigger challenge to a much-loved game. Draw the noughts and crosses grid – two vertical and two horizontal lines – three times vertically down the page. One player is noughts and the other crosses. Take it in turns to draw a symbol onto the grid, with the aim being to get three in a row, either horizontally, vertically or diagonally. But keep an eye on all three grids as now you can score three in a row three-dimensionally.

Crystals

No. of players required: Two

What you will need: Some squared paper and two different-coloured pens.

The simple part: The aim of this game is to grow symmetrical 'crystals' by taking it in turns to colour in two squares at a time on a grid – start with fifteen by fifteen. Players can colour in squares strategically to block other players and stop them from growing their crystals. The larger the crystal, the more points you receive, but the crystal must be symmetrical. Once you are happy with your crystal, you declare it and make a note of the points – then you can no longer add to it.

Did you know?

The world record for the largest pencil drawing by one person measured 98.75 x 2.43 metres and was completed by Ashok Nagpure in 2010 in India.

Triangles

No. of players required: Two

What you will need: A piece of paper, a ruler, pencil and a pen each – these need to be different colours

The simple part: On the piece of paper, draw six dots arranged in the shape of a hexagon and, using the ruler and a pencil, draw straight, faint lines connecting every dot with each of the others, so each dot should have five lines leading from it – this is your board. Players must take it in turns to connect two dots, with the aim being to never form a triangle. Whoever forms a triangle loses the game.

1 2 3 4 5 6 7 8 9 0

Number Games

Fizz-Buzz

Do you have what it takes to fizz and buzz to a hundred?

No. of players required: Four or more – the more the better!

Aim of the game: To make it to as high a number as possible without cracking, and to polish your times tables in the process

How to start: Choose a number to be represented by the word 'fizz' and a number to be represented by 'buzz' – for example, good numbers to go with are three as 'fizz' and five as 'buzz'. All multiples of your chosen numbers will also be represented by these words.

The simple part: Choose a player to start counting and, going round the table, it should play out like this: 'One; two; fizz; four; buzz; fizz; seven; eight; fizz; buzz...' When you reach numbers like fifteen and thirty – multiples of both three and five – you have to make sure you say 'fizz buzz'! In this game it is the players who are able to hold it together who will be triumphant. If you mess up your turn you are out and the game continues with the remaining players. Who will be the Fizz-Buzz champion?

Bingo

*Can you handle the pressure of a
quick-fire game of Bingo?*

No. of players required: Four or more and a caller

Aim of the game: To be the first to cross off all the
numbers on your bingo card

How to start: You'll need some sheets of paper chopped
up into small pieces – on which you need to write the
numbers one to a hundred. It's easier to print out a sheet
of numbers if you can and cut them out. Fold up each
scrap of paper and place in a bowl. Now each player
needs to create a bingo card by drawing a grid of five by
three squares and filling each square with any number
from one to a hundred. Don't repeat any numbers as you
can only cross off one at a time and there will only be
one of each in the bowl.

The simple part: Players will need to take it in turns to be 'caller' for a round of bingo. The caller must select bits of paper from the bowl, one at a time, and read the numbers out for the other players to cross off on their bingo cards. This is best played at great speed. Once a player has crossed off all the numbers on their card they need to shout 'Bingo!' loud and clear – and they win the round. Play best of five or ten or until you're all bingo'd out.

Code Maker, Code Breaker

*Do you have what it takes
to crack your opponent's code?*

No. of players required: Two

Aim of the game: To guess the code maker's four-digit number in just ten moves

How to start: This one takes a little preparation and you'll need to draw up some game sheets first. Use a ruler as a guide and draw a grid of squares comprised of four across and ten down. Then add an extra column on the right-hand side that is twice the width of the other cells. Toss a coin to decide who will be the code maker and who will be the code breaker for the first game. The code maker should write a four-digit number at the bottom of the page – using only the numbers one to eight and avoiding repetition – and fold over the edge of the paper to hide it from their opponent.

The simple part: The code breaker needs to guess the number in just ten tries; they do this by writing a four digit number in one of the rows of the grid and then handing it to the code maker for feedback. If one of the numbers is correct and is also placed correctly in the sequence, a filled-in circle is placed in the extra cell of that row; if one of the numbers matches but is incorrectly placed, an empty circle is drawn in the cell. The code breaker must use the clues from each round to work out the number. Make things more challenging and attempt to crack the code in fewer tries! Play best of five or ten.

Did you know?

There are twenty-five prime numbers between one and 100 — can you list them all?

Function

No. of players required: Two or more

What you will need: A piece of paper and a pen to keep score

The simple part: Players take it in turns to be the caller and the guesser in this game of skill. The guesser starts by saying a number; the caller will have already devised a rule that they will apply to the number offered by the guesser, and will tell the guesser the result but they must keep the rule to themselves. The guesser must then offer another number, and then another, until they work out the rule. For example, if the rule was 'Double the number and add one' and the guesser says 'two', the caller would apply the rule and reply 'five'. Another rule could be the number of letters that appear in the number when spelt out, or the number reversed – for example, 15 becomes 51.

Number Association

No. of players required: Three or more

What you will need: A piece of paper and a pen to keep score

The simple part: Take it in turns to call out a number and the rest of the players must shout out an association with that number – for example, seven might gain the response 'dwarves' or 'deadly sins', while four might obtain 'horsemen of the apocalypse' and twelve might get 'days of Christmas'. Whoever shouts out a correct answer wins a point and any number of answers can be offered up in each round. Keep score and see who fares best.

Pair Up

No. of players required: Two or more

What you will need: A piece of paper and a pen each

The simple part: Write the numbers one to twenty-one all over a sheet of paper – make sure they're jumbled up; then write them a second time on the same piece of paper. Swap sheets and shout 'Go!' The aim of this game is to be the first person to match up all the pairs. It's a simple one, but when played at breakneck speed can be rather fun.

Sevens Catch

No. of players required: Two or more

What you will need: A ball each and an outside space

The simple part: Who said number games were all about rainy days? In this game, players must attempt to be the first to finish, throwing/catching the balls in the seven different ways that follow: throw it against the wall and catch it (seven times); throw it against the wall and catch it after it bounces on the ground (six times); bounce it on the ground and catch it (five times); throw it under your leg, against the wall and catch it (four times); throw it against the wall, let it bounce, hit it back against the wall and catch it (three times); throw it against the wall and touch the ground before catching it (twice); throw it against the wall and turn a full 360 degrees before catching it (once). Everyone got that? Off you go!

Nim

No. of players required: Two

What you will need: Counters or objects – anything will do, but sweets work well

The simple part: Make five piles of sweets – one pile with five sweets, one with four, one with three, one with two and one with just one sweet. Players must take it in turns to remove as many sweets as they wish (but only from one pile). Whoever picks up the final sweet wins the game and gets to eat all the sugary treats. Make things more challenging with more piles and larger numbers of sweets.

Connect Counters

No. of players required: Two

What you will need: A piece of white paper, two sheets of different-coloured paper, a pair of scissors and a 2p coin or similar

The simple part: There's no reason why you can't play this classic game with a homemade board and set of counters. Draw a grid of circles, six down by seven across – draw around a 2 p coin for guidance. Now create 42 counters – 21 of each colour – by drawing around the 2 p. When you have your counters, you're ready to play. Place your counters on the board, one per turn, working from the bottom up. The aim is to achieve four in a row, horizontally, vertically or diagonally.

Number Parade

No. of players required: At least five and maximum eighteen

What you will need: Eighteen sheets of paper and a pen

The simple part: Split into two teams and assign a 'caller'. Each team needs nine sheets of paper on which to write the numbers one to nine, nice and big. The caller will then shout out a number consisting of as many digits as there are players, but with no repetition, for example, 29687; the teams then have to assemble themselves in the right order as quickly as possible. If there aren't nine players per team, each player will have to be responsible for more than one number.

Did you know?

Retired Japanese engineer Akira Haraguchi currently holds the world record for memorising and reciting the most digits of pi. Haraguchi recited 100,000 of the infinite string of digits in sixteen hours in 2005 and hasn't been bettered since.

Reach for the Total

No. of players required: Two or more

What you will need: Some paper and a pen each, and a timer

The simple part: Time to exercise the grey matter. One person should write down two large numbers (25 or 75, for example) and four small numbers (from 1 to 10), while another player should write down a three-digit target number. Players then reveal the numbers to each other and must attempt to reach the target via sums using the numbers provided. Use as many or as few of the numbers as you like, but only use each number once. Give yourselves a minute on the timer. Go!

Battleships

It's sink-or-swim time

No. of players required: Two

Aim of the game: To sink all of your opponent's battleships before they get to yours

How to start: Each player will need two sheets of paper, a pen and a ruler. Using the ruler and pen, draw a decent-sized grid on each piece of paper – say ten by ten squares, with each square being roughly 1 cm squared. Now number your grids down the left-hand side and write letters, starting with 'A', along the top. Without letting your opponent sneak a peek, you need to shade in a few sequences on one of the grids – these are your 'battleships'. You can adapt this game as you see fit, but it tends to be played with five different vessels – one of five shaded squares (positioned horizontally or vertically only), one of four, two of three and one of two squares.

The simple part: Players should take it in turns to guess where the other's battleships might be lurking, by offering up target grid references (for example, B2, E9). This is where you will need your blank grid in order to record your successful and failed attempts to attack your opponent's vessels. It's a race to the finish, so be clever and look for the patterns – whoever sinks all five battleships first wins.

Domino Bingo

Can you survive a night on the tiles?

No. of players required: Two

Aim of the game: To win as many tricks as you possibly can

How to start: You'll need a full set of dominoes and a pen and paper for scoring. All dominoes should be placed face down in the centre; each player should select one to see who goes first (highest number wins) and then one further domino is selected to determine the 'trump' (which cannot be beaten) for the game. Players should then replace the dominoes, leaving the trump tile face up, and select a further seven from the centre. The remaining dominoes become the 'boneyard'.

The simple part: The first player should lay down a tile, while the other should challenge it, attempting to achieve a higher score by adding the two sets of pips together, thus winning the trick. In this game, the blank tile (which is called the 'Bingo') will always win the trick and trumps always beat non-trumps. If no trumps are played, simply add up the pips to determine the winner of the trick. After each trick, the winner should select a domino from the boneyard and lead play. All the while players should be keeping score, adding the pips together and taking into account the special tiles that award extra points – trump double (28), blank tile (14), 0/3 tile (10) and 6/4 (10). When the boneyard is reduced to two dominos, the winner of the previous trick should take the face-up trump tile, while the other player should take the final tile to complete the final trick. Add up the scores to see who has won the game.

Pathways

Can you sneak your way across the board?

No. of players required: Two

Aim of the game: To get from one side of the board to the other without your pesky opponent getting in the way

How to start: For this game you will need a sturdy piece of card, a ruler, pen and some matches or toothpicks. First you need to make your board. Use the ruler and pen to draw a five-by-five-square grid, making sure the sides of each square slightly longer than either the matches or toothpicks you have chosen to use. You should then mark north, south, east and west on the respective sides of the grid. Use a pen to mark two sets of matches or toothpicks in different colours.

The simple part: Each player is given an objective – one must get across the board, forming a continuous line from north to south, while the other must traverse from east to west. Players should take it in turns to lay a matchstick/toothpick on the grid, following the lines, with the aim being to get across the board the fastest without touching the other player's path. The other player will be doing everything they can to block your route and devise their own, so think sharp! Why not try best of five?

Rock, Paper, Scissors

No. of players required: Two

What you will need: Just your hand and a good supply of quick reactions

The simple part: Face your opponent with one hand behind your back. Together, count to three and, on three, show each other your hand formed into a rock, paper or scissors shape. Make a fist for rock, flatten your hand for paper and make a sideways 'V' with your fingers for scissors. Rock blunts scissors, paper wraps rock and scissors cut paper. Try best of three or five to determine the champion.

Did you know?

The game Rock, Paper, Scissors allegedly dates back to the time of the Chinese Han Dynasty (206 BC–AD 220).

Word Builder

No. of players required: Two

What you will need: A few sheets of paper and a pen each

The simple part: Draw a grid of ten by ten squares on a piece of paper and place it in the centre. Now each write out the alphabet on a separate sheet of paper and keep it in front of you. Take it in turns to write words into the grid, intersecting the words like a crossword, crossing off the letters of the alphabet as you use them. Each letter can only be used once and the aim of the game is to be the first to get through the whole alphabet.

So Many Questions!

No. of players required: Two

What you will need: A selection of quick-fire responses

The simple part: Choose a player to start off with a question. This can be anything from 'What do you want to do today?' to 'Why is the sky blue?' The other player must then respond with a question without direct repetition, for example, 'Why do you ask?' or 'Why do you think it is blue?' The aim of the game is to have as lengthy a conversation as possible comprised entirely of questions, with no pauses. Hesitate and you're out!

The Radio Game

No. of players required: Two

What you will need: A radio and a reasonably secluded space

The simple part: This is a game you can play while possibly even playing another game. Have the radio on in the background and wait until a song you know comes on. Take it in turns to sing along for a bit, the other player should then turn the volume right down, while the singer continues singing. The listener should count to ten in their head and then turn the volume back up – has the singer managed to keep in time with the song?

Pick up a Malteser

No. of players required: Two

What you will need: Three plates, two drinking straws and a bag of Maltesers

The simple part: Take a plate each and put it to one side; then place the third plate in-between the two of you. Place a handful of Maltesers onto the plate in the middle and, at the same time, using the straw and your best suction, try to pick up as many of them as possible, transferring them to your own plate. Whoever gets the most wins.

Thumb Wars

No. of players required: Two

What you will need: Strong thumbs

The simple part: There can't be many who don't remember the playground cry, 'One, two, three, four, I declare a thumb war!' It's a classic and requires nothing but a set of sturdy thumbs. Players should face each other and hook the fingers of their right hands together, with their thumbs pointing upwards. Each of you should tap your thumb from left to right and chant the aforementioned thumb war cry. The aim is to topple your opponent's thumb by holding it down and chanting, 'One, two, three, four, I win thumb war!'

Word Pairs

No. of players required: Two

What you will need: A sharp mind

The simple part: One player should start, offering up a pair of words that follow a rule – for example, 'Apples, but not pears', 'Beetles, but not slugs' or 'Football, but not rugby' – and their opponent must guess the rule. Here the rule is double letters together, but you could opt for anything from words beginning with a letter from the first half of the alphabet or words with a certain number of letters. It's fun to pair words that would usually go together but don't in this instance.

Boxes

No. of players required: Two

What you will need: A sheet of paper and a pen each – different colours if possible

The simple part: Draw a grid composed of dots – ten by ten should do. Take it in turns to connect two dots with a line. When you create a box, write your initials inside it and take another turn. The aim of the game is to create as many boxes as possible, while doing everything you can to prevent your opponent from completing any!

Snakes

No. of players required: Two

What you will need: A sheet of paper and a pen each

The simple part: Draw a grid composed of dots – just as you would if you were playing Boxes. Players should take it in turns to connect two dots either horizontally or vertically. The aim of this game is to keep the 'snake' going, without it connecting back to itself – the idea is to force your opponent to do this so you can slither to victory.

Matchboxes

No. of players required: Two

What you will need: A large box of matches or toothpicks and a large, flat surface

The simple part: Lay out the matchsticks in a ten-by-ten-square grid and take it in turns to remove a match each. You may remove two matches if they are touching, either at a right angle or in a straight line, but only one match if it is flying solo. The winner is the person to remove the last match. Liven things up and play it at great speed.

Did you know?

The common balloon was invented by serial inventor Michael Faraday in 1824 and was made from rubber, but the latex versions we know and love were not widely manufactured until 1847.

Indoor Balloon Race

No. of players required: Two

What you will need: Two balloons (and maybe a few spare in case of accidents)

The simple part: Clear a space across the room and perhaps temporarily rehouse any visible breakables in cupboards. This game requires two inflated balloons – one for each player – and the aim of the game is to get to the other side of the room first, with your balloon, but without touching it. Wave your arms about to create a breeze or blow it across the room, but no hands!

Games for Groups

Wink Murder

Knock someone out with that killer look

No. of players required: Five or more

Aim of the game: To 'kill' all other players without being found out

How to start: From a pack of cards, take as many cards as there are players and make sure one is an ace. Each player needs to pick a card; whoever gets the ace is the murderer and the rest are detectives.

The simple part: The murderer must wink at players individually to 'kill' them, without the other players noticing. Once a player has been winked at, they can perform as dramatic and noisy a death as they so choose. Whoever accuses the murderer correctly wins a point and the overall winner is the player with the most points. This game can go on for as long as you like and the more players involved the more fun it is.

Charades

*No speaking is allowed in charades,
so put your best acting hat on*

No. of players required: Two or more

Aim of the game: To guess the film, TV programme, song, etc. being acted out by another player

How to start: Take it in turns to roll a die and see which player should start – highest number starts.

The simple part: To help things along, a selection of suggestions can be written down on slips of paper which are then folded and put into a hat for players to choose from. Use an appropriate action to explain whether you are acting out a song, TV programme or film, etc. Hold up the number of fingers for the number of words in your chosen title; choose which word to start on and either act out that word or if you want to indicate that your action sounds like the word you are acting, cup your hand around your ear.

You can also convey the number of syllables in each word by placing the relevant number of fingers on your forearm. Whoever guesses correctly is up next.

The Post-it Game

*When the answer is almost
staring you in the face*

No. of players required: Two or more

Aim of the game: To guess the name of the famous
person written on a Post-it attached to your forehead

How to start: Each player should write the name of a
famous person on a Post-it and stick it to the forehead of
the player to their left.

The simple part: Players then take it in turns to ask questions about the name on their own forehead. Each question should command only a yes or no answer and if the answer is yes the player may continue asking questions; as soon as the answer is no the player's turn is over and it's the next person's turn to ask questions.

The first player to guess correctly wins a point, but it is fun to keep playing until everyone has guessed the name attached to their forehead.

Did you know?

It would take approximately 507 million Post-it Notes to circle the world once.

Cereal Box Game

No. of players required: Four or more

What you will need: An empty cereal box with the flaps cut off the top

The simple part: Place the box on the floor and, with your arms behind your back, take it in turns to pick up the box with your teeth. After everyone has managed it, cut 1 cm from around the top and repeat. Lean down as far as you can, and one bended knee is acceptable, but one foot must always stay flat on the ground. The winner is the player who can still pick it up without toppling over.

Pass the Parcel

No. of players required: Four or more

What you will need: This game takes preparation – you will need a prize wrapped in many different layers of coloured paper and a means to play music. Additional treats can be slipped in between each layer to keep players interested

The simple part: Pass the parcel around the circle to music (someone needs to be in charge of this); when the music stops, whoever is holding the parcel removes a layer. The winner is the player who unwraps the final layer to reveal the prize.

The Chocolate Bar Game

No. of players required: Three or more

What you will need: A chocolate bar wrapped in several layers of newspaper/wrapping paper and a die, scarf, hat, gloves, knife and fork.

The simple part: Sit in a circle and take it in turns to roll a die; whoever rolls a six must head into the middle of the circle and quickly dress up in all the woollies before trying to get at the chocolate using only the cutlery, not hands. If the player gets through to the chocolate and is able to cut a single piece before another six is thrown by one of the remaining players, they may eat it. Whoever throws the next six picks up where the previous player left off and may tuck into the chocolate using the knife and fork (provided they have dressed up in the woollies) until another six is thrown.

Up Jenkins!

No. of players required: Six or more, there should always be an even number of players

What you will need: One coin

The simple part: Split the players into two teams; whichever team goes first must pass the coin behind their backs to each other while the other team tries to guess who has it in their hand. A player from the opposing team can accuse someone by pointing and shouting 'Up Jenkins!' while the player reveals the contents of their hands. If correct, the accusing team scores a point; if incorrect, the accused team scores a point. Why not play first to five or ten points?

Musical Chairs

No. of players required: Six or more

What you will need: Several chairs – one fewer than there are players – and a means to play music

The simple part: Now here's a classic that never gets old. Arrange the chairs in the centre of the room. Players shuffle around the chairs to music and when the music stops they must find a seat! Whoever doesn't is out and one more chair is taken away.

The Memory Game

No. of players required: Three or more

What you will need: A tray with around 20 small objects on it; paper and a pen for each player, and a bag of treats for prizes

The simple part: Ask players to study the objects for 30 seconds, then cover the items with a cloth and ask them to write down as many as they can remember. The person who names the most items correctly may choose a prize from the bag.

Squeak Piggy Squeak

No. of players required: Six or more

What you will need: One chair fewer than the number of players and a blindfold

The simple part: Players should sit in a circle, with one blindfolded player in the middle. After the blindfolded player has been spun around, they must sit on someone's lap, say 'squeak piggy squeak' and identify the player from their pig squeaking. As soon as they guess correctly, the two players swap roles.

Murder in the Dark

No. of players required: Five or more

What you will need: A pack of cards

The simple part: Remove all but one each of the aces and kings from a deck of cards and distribute evenly among players. Whoever gets the ace is the murderer, and the king the detective. The lights will be switched off for 30 seconds, during which time the murderer must tap one player on the shoulder to 'kill' them. When the lights come back on the detective must guess who the murderer is from the players left 'alive' by asking questions and judging the players' guilt. The detective may only accuse one player of being the murderer; if they guess incorrectly, the light is turned off for another 30 seconds and the murderer gets back to work.

Sardines

No. of players required: Four or more

What you will need: The ability to squeeze into tight spaces

The simple part: It's a case of the more the merrier with sardines. One player hides while the others count to 50. The players then split up to look for the hider and, when they find them, they must join them in their hiding place until all the players but one are crammed in!

Hide and Seek

No. of players required: Three or more

What you will need: A keen sense of a good hiding place

The simple part: This childhood classic can be played with adults too. One player counts to 50 while the others all hide around the house. The counter must then hunt down the other players, who, when found, will one by one join in the search for the remaining hiders. Whoever is discovered last chooses the next counter.

Sleeping Lions

No. of players required: Six or more

What you will need: To perfect the art of stillness

The simple part: Perfect for a bit of after-dinner quiet time. One player is a designated hunter, while the others are sleeping lions. Lions should lie on the floor, perfectly still, while the hunter should tell jokes and pull faces to provoke a reaction. Once a lion has reacted, they become a hunter and the winner is the last player left 'sleeping'.

Blind Man's Bluff

No. of players required: Four or more

What you will need: A blindfold

The simple part: This game may require breakables to be hidden out of reach. One player should be blindfolded and spin around, while the others scatter around the room; then the 'blind' player tries to catch them. Once caught, the blindfolded player must guess who they have taken prisoner. If they guess correctly they can then swap places.

Did you know?

In Victorian England, while the blindfolded player was being spun around they would be asked how many horses their father had – to which they would reply 'Three', before being asked 'What colour are they?', to which they would further reply 'Black, white and grey', before everyone shouted 'Turn around three times and catch who you may!'

Games for Around the Dinner Table

Botticelli

Flex your knowledge of both famous and fictional figures

No. of players required: Four or more

Aim of the game: To guess the famous person or fictional character your opponent is thinking of – with only the initial of their surname to go on. To do this, you must ask them direct and indirect questions, but you are only permitted to ask a direct question if you have earned it.

How to start: Whoever is taking their turn should offer up the initial of the surname of the person they are thinking of. The rest of the players must then take it in turns to ask indirect questions relating to individuals who share that initial in the hope they will stumble upon the correct answer. For example, if the initial was 'B' you might ask: 'Did you write *Wuthering Heights*?', 'Did you sing about the "Bare Necessities"?' or 'Are you a former Labour prime minister?'. The first two can only have one answer (Emily Brontë and Baloo, respectively), but the answer to the third question could be either Tony Blair or Gordon Brown.

The simple part: If the player taking a turn is unable to answer your indirect question, you must give them the answer and are then permitted to ask a direct question with a yes or no answer – such as 'Are you female?', 'Are you fictional?', 'Are you British?', 'Are you in the arts?', etc. As the aim is to ask as many direct questions as possible, why not make the indirect questions tricky? Whoever correctly guesses the name of the person then takes their turn.

Did you know?

The game Botticelli is named so because the chosen subject should be at least as well known as its namesake – Italian early Renaissance painter Sandro Botticelli.

Psychiatrist

*Try not to lose any friends in
this game of mimicry*

No. of players required: Six or more

Aim of the game: To guess who exactly of the other
people in the room a player is attempting to mimic

How to start: Choose someone to be the 'psychiatrist'
and send them out of the room. Write down the names
of the remaining players on separate slips of paper, fold
them and place in a hat or bowl. Each player should take
a piece of paper and has to pretend that they believe they
are that person.

The simple part: Once the 'psychiatrist' returns to the room, they will ask each player a question in turn. The players will respond as if they were the other player written on their slip of paper. From their behaviour, mannerisms and answers, the 'psychiatrist' must guess which player they are doing an impression of.

An alternative here is to choose a famous person, for example, Elvis Presley or Michael Jackson, whom all the remaining players must mimic.

Alphabet Conversation

*Can you successfully take
the chatter from A to Z?*

No. of players required: Four or more

Aim of the game: To let conversation flow around the table with each player's contribution starting with the next letter of the alphabet.

How to start: Either take it in turns to roll a dice or start with the youngest. Whoever kicks things off needs to turn to the player on their left and start a conversation beginning with the letter 'A' – for example, they might say: 'Are you enjoying your meal?' The player to the left must then form a response that begins with 'B' – for example, they might say: 'But of course!' The next player to the left must carry things on – all the while keeping an eye on the alphabet – and might say: 'Can we get things moving, I'm nearly ready for dessert.'

The simple part: A typical conversation might continue a little something like this:

'Do you think you can wait a moment?'

'Entertaining, isn't this?'

'Fascinating stuff, dinner party banter.'

'Good to know I'm not the only one who thinks so.'

'He might think so too.'

'I certainly agree with you.'

'Just think, what would we do without these sorts of social occasions?'

And so on! Try going through the alphabet twice for more of a challenge.

Hello Harry

No. of players required: Six or more

What you will need: A table of people up for a very repetitive, but also most amusing game of greetings.

The simple part: Choose a player to start. This player should turn to his left and say 'Hello Harry', to which the greeted player should respond 'Yes, Harry?' and be told by the starting player 'Tell Harry'. That player then turns to their left and repeats the conversation. This goes on until someone slips up – players can mutter their greeting in a different direction to catch someone out, for example – and has to become Brian, then Albert, then Dipwick. This game gets interesting when more names other than Harry are thrown into the mix and it becomes a challenge to remember who's who!

Secret Messages

No. of players required: Six or more

What you will need: A healthy knowledge of song titles, some paper and a pen

The simple part: This game takes a bit of preparation, but it's worth it. Write a song title on a piece of paper for each person sitting at the table and slip it underneath their plate – for example, 'Let's Get Ready to Rhumble', 'You're So Vain', 'Welcome to the Jungle'. Each diner must slip their song title into conversation throughout the course of the meal without the other players noticing. If another player does notice, they can say so and have their guess confirmed or denied. The last to have their song title spotted is the winner.

Freeze!

No. of players required: Six or more

What you will need: To remain perfectly still

The simple part: Another simple one, all we need here is for players to decide on the game and then go about their conversations, etc., as before. One player will then freeze into position, staying perfectly still in the pose of their choosing – but the key is to be subtle. As players notice, they too should freeze and the last to do so is out of the game.

Twenty Questions

No. of players required: Four or more

What you will need: A sharp mind and quick responses

The simple part: Choose a player to start. This player should think of an object – anything from a potato to Horatio Nelson's hat, Bart Simpson's skateboard, a lorry or a walnut – and tell the other players whether it is animal, vegetable or mineral. The other players must then ask questions with yes or no answers and guess before they hit twenty questions. Whoever successfully guesses the object takes a turn.

The Yes/No Game

No. of players required: Two or more
What you will need: The ability to think your way out of the answer your opponent wants you to give

The simple part: This game is pretty simple: choose a player to start and all other players should start firing questions at them. The only rule: no 'yes' or 'no' answers allowed! The moment a player cracks and answers either 'yes' or 'no', their turn is over and whoever caught them out is up.

Fantasy Music Festival

No. of players required: Four or more

What you will need: A decent knowledge of bands or artists past or present

The simple part: Going around the table, whoever goes first should start off by saying, 'I'm going to a music festival, you'll never guess who's playing...', then naming a band/singer/artist beginning with 'A', for example, Adele or Abba. The player to the left should then repeat, building on the line-up by adding a band/singer/artist beginning with 'B'. The aim of the game is to get to 'Z', successfully remembering the entire line-up as you go.

Thumbs

No. of players required: Six or more

What you will need: A degree in the art of subtlety

The simple part: All players should decide to start the game and then simply get on with the meal, acting as before. The aim of the game is to place your thumb over the edge of the table by your side without anyone noticing. One by one, players will notice and, without drawing attention to themselves, should do the same. The last person to place their thumb on the table must sit out the next round.

Spots

No. of players required: Four or more

What you will need: A few sheets of stickers – red dots are ideal, but any colour will do – and a place card for each guest with a silly, made up name on it (for example, Captain Mouldy Socks or Professor Green Eggs)

The simple part: Guests must make sure they refer to each other by their made-up name. If anyone is caught referring to someone by their real name they must take a sticker and stick it to their face. As the evening goes on everyone will start to look more and more silly.

Left Hand Only

No. of players required: Four or more

What you will need: You can use the stickers from your game of Spots quite successfully

The simple part: At the start of the meal, explain the rules to the table: everyone must use their left hand to pick up their glass for the rest of the evening and anyone caught using their right must take a sticker to the face. Whoever has the most stickers on their face at the end of the meal has lost the game – why not introduce a forfeit?

How's Your French?

No. of players required: Four or more

What you will need: Pens, paper and at least a basic grasp of French

The simple part: Take a pen and paper and write down a few words or a sentence in French. Pass the piece of paper to your left and let the next player translate. Fold over the paper to conceal the original French words and let the next player translate the English back into French. Carry this on until everyone has had a turn and then unfold the paper to see how good (or bad) everyone's translation skills are!

Keep a Straight Face

No. of players required: Two or more

What you will need: The strength not to laugh

The simple part: Whoever's turn it is must keep a straight face while the rest of the players do everything in their power to make them laugh. No tickling allowed here as physical contact is forbidden and it's words only. As soon as a player laughs it's the next person's turn.

Did you know?

Laughter has been found to relax our muscles, help us cope with stress and boost our self-esteem, so play this game regularly!

OUTDOOR GAMES

What's the Time, Mr Wolf?

*You don't want to hear the words
'dinner time' when playing this game...*

No. of players required: Four or more

Aim of the game: To reach the wall without being caught
by Mr Wolf

How to start: All you need for this one is a bit of space and a wall. Choose a player to be Mr Wolf. This player should stand facing the wall, while the others face in the same direction 20 paces away.

The simple part: Players take it in turns to ask Mr Wolf the time and take steps towards him according to his replies, e.g. 5 o'clock = five steps, 12 o'clock = 12 steps. Mr Wolf can, at any time of his choosing, announce it to be 'dinner time!' and turn to grab or chase the players, depending on how close to him they are. The first player to be caught then becomes Mr Wolf and the game continues.

Capture the Flag

Can you lead your team to victory?

No. of players required: Eight or more

Aim of the game: To capture the other team's flag and bring it back to your own territory without getting caught

How to start: This one works best with lots of players and a decent-sized garden or area of a park. Players are split into two teams and each team has five minutes to hide their flag (a tea towel will do) on their designated half of the playing area. Each team should also choose a base area. You should be able to see a bit of the flag poking out from its hiding place and it should be easy enough to grab, so don't bury it or tie it to anything.

The simple part: Players should try their hardest to get hold of the other team's flag – by hiding behind trees, crawling on their hands and knees, and generally being swift as anything – and bring it back to their base without being tagged by a member of the other team. If you do get caught, you get put in 'prison' (a designated patch of grass) but can be freed at the touch of one of your team members. Whoever gets back to base first with the other team's flag and their team intact wins.

Apple Bobbing and Marshmallows in Flour

Things are about to get messy...

No. of players required: Two or more

Aim of the game: Enjoy yourself and eat what you can

How to start: For these two timeless activities, you need two large bowls – one filled with water and apples, and the other filled with marshmallows and flour. You guessed it, this one is about to get silly.

The simple part: This is traditionally played on Halloween in the States, but there's no reason why it doesn't suit a dull Sunday afternoon too. With your hands behind your back, bob for the apple first. Once you've got your teeth into one of those juicy morsels, take a big bite (still no hands!) and then head for the marshmallows. Hoover up as many of the marshmallows as you can, while the flour turns to a delightful paste on your face. The winner in this game is simply the fullest and messiest.

String Doughnuts

No. of players required: Two or more

What you will need: A washing line, a ball of string and some ring doughnuts

The simple part: Simply tie the doughnuts to the washing line, making sure they dangle enough for players to reach them, and watch players attempt to eat them with their hands behind their backs. Try various lengths of string to make things more interesting. No licking your lips either!

Did you know?

American Hanson Gregory claimed to have invented the ring doughnut in 1847 when he was just 16. Gregory alleged he became dissatisfied with the doughy centre of regular doughnuts so punched a hole through the centre with a tin pepper box to fix the problem.

Pin the Tail on the Donkey

No. of players required: Four or more

What you will need: This classic party game requires a picture of a donkey – or anything with a tail really – attached to a cork board and a 'tail' (a cut elastic band or tea towel, perhaps) with a pin attached to it.

The simple part: Players take it in turn to be blindfolded and, tail in hand, get as close as possible to the spot where the tail should be. The winner is the player who places the tail the closest.

Three-Legged Race

No. of players required: Six or more (must be an even number)

What you will need: An old rag per pair

The simple part: This sports-day classic never fails to entertain all players involved. Grab a partner and, using an old rag or something reasonably soft, tie your left and their right leg together. Now you have three legs between you. Players should line up with their partners and race the other three-legged players. Whoever crosses the line first wins.

Piñata

No. of players required: Two or more

What you will need: First you need a papier-mâché piñata (you can either make or buy one of these) filled with plenty of sweets, a large stick or rounders bat and a blindfold

The simple part: Blindfolded players take it in turns to use the stick to attempt to hit the piñata, which is suspended from a tree. The winner is the player who nabs the treats.

40–40

No. of players required: Four or more

What you will need: Lots of energy

The simple part: Choose a player to be seeker and choose a base. The seeker stands on the base and counts to 40 while the other players hide. The seeker must spot the hiders and run back to base to announce their name and whereabouts to catch them out. If a player gets back to base without being seen they shout '40–40 home'. The last hider can save everyone if they do this and shout '40–40 save all'.

Water Balloon Relay Race

No. of players required: Four or more

What you will need: Lots of water balloons

The simple part: Now here's one for the warmer summer months. Split into teams of no fewer than two and no more than four. Decide at the start how many laps you want to do. Players must carry a water balloon from one side of the garden/field to the other without using their hands. Once they reach the other side, they tag their teammate who carries it back again.

Slow Bicycle Race

No. of players required: Two or more

What you will need: A bicycle each and a sense of steadiness

The simple part: Create a start and finish line for the race, and add a few obstacles if you feel that way inclined. The aim of the game is to ride your bicycle as slowly as possible, without falling off or letting your feet touch the ground. Unlike most of the other games here, the last over the finish line wins!

Paint Can Race

No. of players required: Two or more

What you will need: Two old paint cans each, with some sturdy string tied to the can, through two holes pierced in the top, long enough for you to hold on to while standing up

The simple part: Create a start and a finish line. Stand on the paint cans and take the string in your hands. The aim of the game is to use the paint cans as stilts and race each other to the finish line. First one there wins. If there are loads of you, why not try a paint-can relay race?

Tug of War

No. of players required: Two or more (but really you need as many as possible)

What you will need: A very long and sturdy piece of rope, a handkerchief and all the strength you can muster

The simple part: Split into teams of an even number. If there's an odd number of you, perhaps people can take it in turns to be umpire. Lay the rope on the ground and find the middle; tie the handkerchief here and create a marker on the ground which marks the point you want to pull the opposing team over. Line up at each end of the rope and, at 'go', pull with all your might. The team to pull a player over to their side of the marker first wins.

Conkers

No. of players required: Initially two, but any more and you could have a tournament

What you will need: The best conker you can find and about 25-30 cm of string. Using a skewer, make a hole through the centre of the conker and thread the string through it, making a knot at the end.

The simple part: Two players should face each other and, holding the end of the string, take it in turns to use their own conker to try to crack or break their opponent's. The last conker standing is the winner.

Welly Throwing

No. of players required: Two or more (the more the better so you all feel silly together)

What you will need: One welly per player and a large open space

The simple part: Make a line on the ground from where you will be launching your wellies. Take it in turns to throw your trusty wellington boot as far as you possibly can – overarm, underarm or any way you please. Once all wellies have been thrown, walk over to the boots to find out who threw theirs the furthest and they will be pronounced the winner. Try best of five. Mark your initials on the sole of your welly just in case everyone's look the same!

Games to Play in the Car

The Movie Game

Where your knowledge of the big screen comes into play

No. of players required: Three or more

Aim of the game: To keep the movie chain going for as long as possible

How to start: The player starting off the game should pick a film, for example, *Harry Potter and the Chamber of Secrets*, while the next player must name an actor from that film, which in this case could be Daniel Radcliffe.

The simple part: The next player must then name another film that actor has appeared in – *The Woman in Black* would be a probable answer here – and the chain continues until a player is stumped. Sequels are acceptable, but only when the full film title is given, for example, *Terminator 2: Judgment Day*. Whoever breaks the chain must take the letter 'M', then 'O', then 'V', 'T', 'E' and 'S'; the first to reach 'MOVIES' is out of the game. You can be as obscure as you like here, but know your audience – no game is any fun if the others aren't enjoying themselves.

Word Chain

*Impress the other players with
your specialist subject*

No. of players required: Three or more

Aim of the game: To keep the word chain going for as
long as possible

How to start: Take it in turns to choose a broad subject,
for example, food, band names, place names, animals, etc.
– make sure you have a good knowledge of your chosen
subject matter.

The simple part: Whoever has chosen should start with something from that subject, for example, with places, you might say 'London'; the next player then has to respond with a place name beginning with the last letter, so in this case 'Nevada' or 'Nice' would be appropriate. If your chosen answer begins and ends with the same letter, for example, 'Tibet' or 'Alabama', the direction of play changes. If a player hesitates for too long or can't come up with an answer, they must take the letter 'W', then 'O', 'R' and 'D', and when they reach this they are out of the game. If you'd rather play a longer game, simply spell out 'WORD CHAIN', or anything you like really.

Just A Minute

You'll need the gift of the gab for this game

No. of players required: Two or more

Aim of the game: To talk fluidly about a specific topic for at least one minute

How to start: Give each player a piece of paper and a pen, and ask them to write down five different topics. Tear the paper, so each topic is on a separate piece; gather all the pieces, fold them up and place into a hat or bowl. Choose a player to be the timekeeper – either use a watch or find the stopwatch function on your mobile phone; this way you can set an alarm to go off after sixty seconds.

The simple part: Players should take it in turns to pick a topic from the hat and talk about it for at least one minute. In order to make this challenging, there must be no hesitation, repetition or deviation. Players who stray from the subject at hand will be penalised. If you are successful, you should hold on to your scrap of paper – these will be counted up at the end to see who is verbally victorious.

Did you know?

Just A Minute is best known as the basis of the long-running BBC Radio 4 comedy panel game in which contestants must talk for one minute on a given subject, without hesitating, repeating or deviating.

Grandma's Picnic

No. of players required: Two or more

What you will need: A very good memory

The simple part: The player chosen to start should say, 'I went to Grandma's picnic and I brought...' followed by one picnic item – this could be sausage rolls, sandwiches, jelly, cakes, a Frisbee, a football, etc. Players take it in turns to add items – reciting the growing list on each turn – and the aim is to make it as long as possible. If a player forgets an item or the order of the list, they must sit out until the next game.

I Spy

No. of players required: Two or more

What you will need: An eagle eye

The simple part: The player whose turn it is should choose an object or landmark, either inside or outside the car, and provide the other players with the first letter, saying, 'I spy with my little eye something beginning with...' Whatever you choose, make sure it will be visible long enough for the other players to guess. Make things more interesting by spying two-word objects, for example cats' eyes, and give your opponents two letters – in this instance 'CE'.

Name That Tune

No. of players required: Three or more

What you will need: An ear for a tune and good musical knowledge

The simple part: Whoever goes first should either hum or, if that's just too easy, tap, whistle (or even belch) out a tune for the other players to guess. The first player to guess the tune correctly then steps up to take a turn delivering a 'musical' number. Make things more interesting and choose a theme or a musical genre to stick to.

What Am I?

No. of players required: Two or more

What you will need: A keen, inquisitive mind

The simple part: The first player to start should choose something their opponents can guess by asking yes or no questions. You can choose anything from a badger to a bath mat, while other players ask: 'Are you hairy?', 'Are you edible?', 'Are you useful?' etc. Whoever guesses correctly takes a turn. Make things a bit more challenging by setting a limit to the number of questions players can ask.

The Number Plate Game

No. of players required: One or more (it'll always be more fun with at least two of you)

What you will need: Eyes like a hawk

The simple part: This one is terribly simple and yet can entertain a carload of people for miles. First of all, look for a car that features the letter 'A' on its number plate; next you need to find 'B', then 'C', until you've completed the alphabet. Players should shout (but not so loudly you disturb the driver!) when they spot the next letter in the sequence and whoever spies the most wins.

Once Upon a Time

No. of players required: Two or more

What you will need: A healthy imagination

The simple part: One player should start: 'Once upon a time...' and continue the sentence to start off the story, for example, '... there was a man who lived in a lighthouse...' The next player should repeat the start of the story and add to the sentence, for example, '... who liked to eat sardine and egg sandwiches...' Players must remember the story, adding to it each time and keeping it going for as long as possible.

Traffic Lights

No. of players required: Two or more

What you will need: To be driving through an area with a reasonable number of traffic lights

The simple part: Before you start the game, everyone must make their guess: how many traffic lights will the car pass through on green before it is stopped at a red? Make a guess and pronounce the game officially in session – and just see what happens. Play as many rounds as you like and whoever has made the most correct guesses wins.

Mystery Writing

No. of players required: Two

What you will need: A heightened sense of touch

The simple part: All good car games should require minimal tools and this game is no exception. Simply take it in turns to spell out words by drawing letters on the palm of a player's hand with one finger. Can you guess what your opponent is writing? Keep the words short to begin with and if you're being drawn on, keep your eyes closed!

What Am I Counting?

No. of players required: Two or more

What you will need: A set of eagle eyes

The simple part: Whoever starts should choose something outside the car that they can count – for example, cows, red cars, lampposts, etc. – but they mustn't tell anyone what they're counting. Each time they spot one of their chosen objects/animals, they should count loudly. The other players simply have to guess what it is they're counting. Don't be too obscure or there won't be much counting to do!

Treasure Hunt

No. of players required: Two or more

What you will need: A pre-written list of objects/animals/ sights to spot from the car window and something to write with

The simple part: Each player should have the same list in front of them, featuring things like: brown dog, fire engine, someone with an umbrella, roadworks, church, etc. The first to spot everything on the list wins the game.

Spoof

No. of players required: Three or more

What you will need: Each player will need three coins

The simple part: Each player puts both hands behind their back and decides how many coins they want to play the round with. Once everyone has decided, each player must guess the total number of coins being 'played'. You can't guess the same number as anyone else, so take it in turns to guess first. The winner is the player who guesses closest. The more players the better in this game – it'll make guessing more challenging.

Next Car

No. of players required: Two or more

What you will need: To be travelling down reasonably quiet, winding roads

The simple part: Each player should guess the colour of the next car to come round the corner; each correct guess wins a point. When you get bored of colours, why not guess the make of the car? Or you could devise a points system: two points for a caravan, four points for a coach, ten points for a horsebox, etc.

Don't Forget!

Whoever is driving needs to keep their eyes on the road, so try to only involve them in the games that don't require much scanning of the landscape.

If you're interested in finding out more
about our books, find us on Facebook at
Summersdale Publishers and follow us on
Twitter at **@Summersdale**.

www.summersdale.com